PUFFINS

Amy-Jane Beer

Grolier
an imprint of

www.scholastic.com/librarypublishing

Published 2008 by Grolier
An imprint of Scholastic Library Publishing
Old Sherman Turnpike, Danbury,
Connecticut 06816

For The Brown Reference Group plc
Project Editor: Jolyon Goddard
Copy-editors: Lesley Ellis, Lisa Hughes,
    Wendy Horobin
Picture Researcher: Clare Newman
Designers: Jeni Child, Lynne Ross,
    Sarah Williams
Managing Editor: Bridget Giles

Volume ISBN-13: 978-0-7172-6260-1
Volume ISBN-10: 0-7172-6260-X

**Library of Congress
Cataloging-in-Publication Data**

Nature's children. Set 2.
    p. cm.
  Includes bibliographical references and
  index.
  ISBN-13: 978-0-7172-8081-0
  ISBN-10: 0-7172-8081-0
  1. Animals--Encyclopedias, Juvenile. I.
  Grolier (Firm)
  QL49.N383 2007
  590--dc22
                    2007026928

Printed and bound in China

PICTURE CREDITS

Front Cover: **Shutterstock**: Thomas
O'Neal

Back Cover: **Nature PL**: Louis Gagnon,
Chris Gomersall, Solvin Zankl;
Shutterstock: Joe Gough

Alamy: Les Gibbon 45, James Osmond 30;
Corbis: Annie Poole/Papilio 46; **FLPA**: Mike
Jones 34, 37; **Nature PL**: Nigel Bean 42;
NHPA: Joe Blosom 41, Bill Coster 18;
Photolibrary.com: Johnny Johnson 38;
Shutterstock: Joe Gough 14, 21, Gail
Johnson 2–3, 22, Eric Krveger 9, Franziska
Lang 17, Thomas O'Neil 6, Steffen Foerster
Photography 10, Noah Strycker 33, Jerome
Whittingham 4, 5, 13; **Still Pictures**:
BIOS/Bily Guillume 29, BIOS/Christophe
Perelle 26–27.

Contents

Fact File: Puffins 4

Auks and Penguins 7

Three of a Kind 8

Clown Faces 11

The Missing Toe 12

Seafood Supper 15

Clear the Way! 16

Dive, Dive, Dive! 19

Warm and Dry 20

Seabird Cities 23

By the Thousands 24

Mr. and Mrs. Puffin 25

Feature Photo 26–27

Making a Home 28

Fights and Scuffles 31

Puffin Talk 32

The Egg Arrives 35

Early Days 36

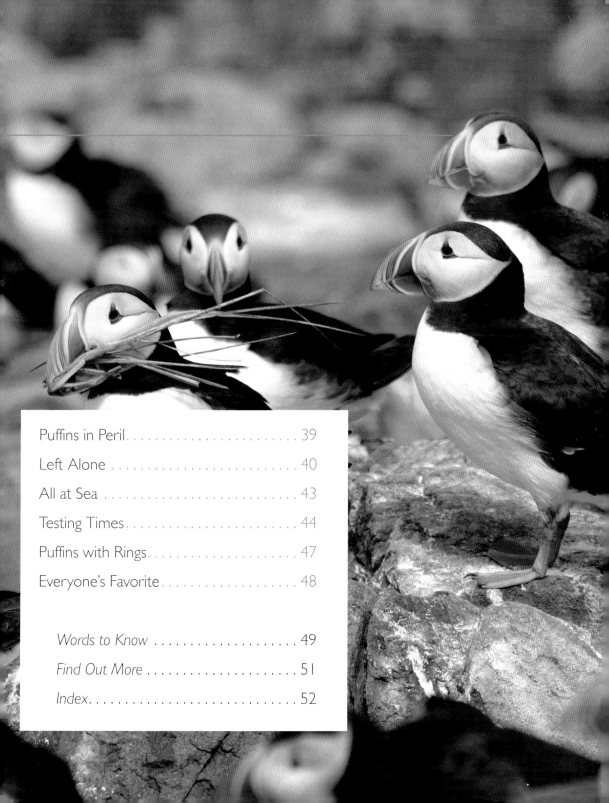

Puffins in Peril. 39

Left Alone 40

All at Sea 43

Testing Times. 44

Puffins with Rings. 47

Everyone's Favorite 48

Words to Know 49

Find Out More 51

Index. 52

FACT FILE: Puffins

Class	Birds (Aves)
Order	Plovers, sandpipers, gulls, terns, and auks (Charadriiformes)
Family	Puffins (Alcidae)
Genus	Puffins (*Fratercula*)
Species	Three species, including the Atlantic puffin (*Fratercula arctica*)
World distribution	Northern parts of the Atlantic and Pacific Oceans
Habitat	Open ocean, nest in summer on low cliffs with grassy tops
Distinctive physical characteristics	Stout body, striking black and white plumage, large feet, and large colorful beak in the breeding season
Habits	Pair for life, breed in burrows on land, and spend the rest of the year at sea
Diet	Fish, crustaceans, and squid

Introduction

Do you know which birds are sometimes called sea parrots? With their large colorful beak and comical upright stance, puffins have as much personality and charm as tropical parrots—and they can be almost as noisy, too. But that is where the similarities end. Unlike puffins, you won't see a parrot eating fish, bobbing around on an icy ocean, or "flying" underwater like a speeding submarine!

Puffins live for up to 15 years. They spend most of their life far out to sea. But every summer they come ashore for a few months to breed.

An Atlantic puffin squats on a rock.

The common
Atlantic puffin
has a stout body,
a short neck,
and a large beak.

Auks and Penguins

Puffins belong to a family of birds known as **auks** (ORKS). Auks are seabirds that breed on land, but eat fish from the sea. They are all excellent underwater swimmers. Most auks have a stout body, a short neck, a short tail, a large beak, big feet, and black and white feathers. In all of these ways, auks are very much like penguins. Both types of birds have a body shape that is well suited for diving underwater and catching fish. Despite their many similarities, penguins and auks are not related. Penguins live in the southern **hemisphere**, while most auks live in the northern hemisphere.

Three of a Kind

There are three different **species**, or types, of puffins. They can all be seen on the coasts of North America. The first species is the common Atlantic puffin. Its scientific name is *Fratercula arctica*. The word *fratercula* means "little brother" in Latin. Scientists chose this name because they thought these birds looked like little monks, and monks always call one another "Brother." The *arctica* part of the name comes from the Arctic, where the puffins live.

The second species of puffin is the Pacific horned puffin, *Fratercula corniculata*. It has small fleshy horns growing just above its eyes. *Corniculata* is Latin for "with little horns."

The last species of puffin is the Pacific tufted puffin, *Fratercula cirrhata*. The tufted puffin is the largest puffin species. It has tufts of long yellow feathers on its head.

Pacific tufted puffins have long yellow feathers on their head during the breeding season.

9

Reddish orange, dark blue, and yellow—the puffin's beak cannot be missed during the breeding season.

Clown Faces

People often say that puffins look like little clowns. They stand up straight, have a comical way of walking, and they make unusual sounds. But most clownlike of all is their face. They look as though their face has been carefully painted white, with the sad eyes of an old-fashioned clown. In the breeding season, puffins also have a spectacular reddish orange, dark blue, and yellow beak. The beak is so big—in relation to the size of the bird—that it looks as though it could be fake. This amazingly colored beak lasts only for the breeding season. In winter it is much smaller and its colors are dull.

The Missing Toe

Puffins and other auks have large, **webbed feet**, which make great paddles when they swim. The feet also act as air brakes when the puffin is flying. If you watch a puffin coming in to land, you'll see it lift its feet in front of its body, just like the flaps on an airplane's wings as it approaches a runway. A puffin's feet are bright orange. The color is brightest in summer.

There is something else unusual about a puffin's feet. Most birds have three long toes at the front of their foot and a short toe at the back. But the puffin does not have a back toe at all. The same is true for all auks. That partly explains why they wobble as they walk! There is no back toe to help them keep their balance.

Although all puffins have three front toes on each foot, they do not have a back toe.

This common
Atlantic puffin
has caught a
bunch of sand eels.

Seafood Supper

Puffins eat all kinds of seafood. Sand eels are their favorite, perhaps because their long, thin shape allows a puffin to carry more in one beakful than any other sort of fish. But if sand eels are not available, puffins will happily eat other fish, such as smelts, haddock, and baby cod, as well as small squid, crabs, and shrimps.

How can a puffin hold so many fish in its mouth and still catch more? The secret lies in the puffin's tongue. The tongue has lots of tiny spikes on it that help grip the slippery bodies of the fish. While the tongue is holding onto the puffin's catch, the bird uses its beak to add more fish to its stockpile!

Clear the Way!

Puffins are not graceful fliers. Compared with the lazy, drifting flight of many other seabirds, puffins look a bit frantic. Their wings are small, so they have to flap them very fast to stay aloft.

The hardest part of flying is taking off. To lift off from water, the puffin paddles as fast as it can with its wings whirring. But it sometimes needs several attempts to get airborne. It's easier to take off from cliff tops, where puffins use the edge as a launch pad. Usually there are updrafts of air at the cliff face that help them on their way.

Landing is easier, but never very controlled. Often, puffins seem to simply plop into the sea. Their cliff-top landings usually involve a bounce and a stumble—with other birds scrambling to get out of the way!

An Atlantic puffin puts a lot of effort into taking off.

A Pacific tufted puffin swims swiftly underwater, hunting for fish.

Dive, Dive, Dive!

Underwater, puffins look completely different from the frantic flapping animals of the air. Suddenly, all traces of their clumsiness are gone, and they zoom through the water like torpedoes. They use their wings as propellers and their feet and tail to steer. Their short fat body straightens out, becoming almost **streamlined**. The huge beak becomes a deadly fish trap.

The fish dart this way and that, but the puffin is just as quick on the turns. The bird is also smart enough to guess which way the fish will go next. Snapping its beak, a puffin collects one fish after another in a single dive—and there always seems to be room for one more fish in its beak.

Warm and Dry

Puffins look plump, but if you picked one up you'd be surprised by how light it is. Most of the bird's bulk is feathers. The feathers on the outside are smooth and greasy. They do a great job of keeping the bird dry, even when the puffin dives underwater. These outer feathers act a little like a diver's drysuit. Beneath the waterproof feathers is a thick layer of much fluffier feathers. These under feathers trap a layer of warm, dry air close to the puffin's skin, so even when the bird dives it never gets really wet.

The only problem is that all the air in the feathers makes the puffin float very easily. That is ideal when the puffin just wants to bob around on the surface of the sea. But when the puffin wants to dive, it has to work hard to stay underwater.

Puffins have waterproof outer feathers that help keep them dry.

A colony of puffins starts to build nests on its cliff-top home.

Seabird Cities

In spring and summer, puffins set up home on cliff tops and islands. Some places have just a few puffins. But the best nesting places can have tens of thousands of these birds. They don't really choose to live together, rather they all know where the best places are to raise their families. It's like people choosing to live in a large, noisy city. They live there not because they like the noise and crowds, but because that is where they can best make a living. These seabird cities are called **colonies**.

Like human cities, seabird colonies have many different characters. Puffins usually live on the grassy cliff tops, while other birds live on the cliff face itself. Gannets and fulmars nest on the broad ledges, for example, and gulls such as kittiwakes build their nests on the narrow ones. Razorbills, guillemots (GHI-LUH-MOTS), and cormorants nest lower down, on ledges and boulders near the cliff bottom.

By the Thousands

The world's largest puffin nesting colonies
are usually situated on small islands where the
puffins are safe from predators, such as foxes,
stoats, and rats. At Witless Bay, Newfoundland,
there are more than a quarter of a million pairs
of Atlantic puffins jostling for space on four
small islands. On the other side of the Atlantic
Ocean, the birds are even more tightly packed.
The tiny Scottish island of St Kilda is home to
a mind-boggling 300,000 pairs of puffins. They
are all crammed into an area about twice the size
of Central Park. As if that wasn't crowded
enough, the island is also home to the world's
largest colony of gannets and tens of thousands
of fulmars, razorbills, and gulls. Imagine the
noise—and the smell! Those cliffs are completely
covered in fishy bird droppings!

Mr. and Mrs. Puffin

Puffins usually choose a **mate** when they are young and they stay together for life. Like all "married couples," they sometimes squabble. But they both work hard to look after each other and to defend and care for their young.

At the start of the breeding season, when the puffins arrive at the nesting site, both the males and females are in breeding colors. The beak turns reddish orange, dark blue, and yellow, and their feet turn a brighter shade of orange. Puffin pairs spend a lot of time together **courting**. They nibble and nuzzle each other and rub and rattle their beaks together. They also call to each other all the time.

Nuzzling their beaks, a pair of courting puffins get to know each other.

26

Making a Home

Puffins rear their young in a burrow, just like rabbits. In fact, rabbits and puffins sometimes use one another's burrows. They both like to burrow in the same types of sandy soils, which drain well and are easy to dig. Puffins dig with their beak and their feet. Each of the three toes on both feet has a sharp claw that helps loosen the soil. The webbing between each toe acts as a shovel to toss out the soil. There's no need for nesting puffins to build a new burrow every year. But at the start of the season there's usually a bit of tidying up to do.

Puffins often collect bits of plant or feathers as though they plan to make a nest. But when they get them home, they seem to forget what they are for. Quite often, their single egg is laid on the bare dirt floor.

An Atlantic puffin peers out from the entrance to its burrow.

Wings flapping and beaks snapping, rival puffins fight for space and burrows.

Fights and Scuffles

At the start of the breeding season, when puffins arrive at their nesting sites, there is always a lot of fighting over which pairs get the best burrows.

Puffins growl and use body language to drive others away. They open their beak wide, as though they are yawning. If the intruder doesn't back down, the puffin rushes at it and tries to grab the beak of the **trespasser** with its own. With their beaks clamped together, the rivals push and shove and use their wings to try and knock each other over. Cliff tops are dangerous places for this type of rough and tumble. Sometimes both puffins end up rolling over the edge.

31

Puffin Talk

A puffin colony can be a noisy place. It doesn't seem to matter if they are calm or angry, contented or worried, puffins are constantly making a noise.

A puffin sitting peacefully on its egg makes a long, low "aa-aa-aa-aa" call, almost like a lullaby. When the other parent arrives, the two puffins greet each other with a purring noise. When a puffin is alarmed, it might give a short sharp "ha-ha!" Then there is the sound used to scare away other birds—a harsh, threatening "uuur." This is the puffin version of a growl. From a distance, all of these calls blend together. To human ears, the puffin colony can sound like a room full of people muttering, chatting, laughing, and shrieking!

An Atlantic puffin calls out to its mate.

33

A single puffin egg rests in a simple grassy nest.

The Egg Arrives

After the male and female puffin have mated, the female lays one large egg in the burrow. The egg is white, with brown or purple spots at the wide end. The parents take turns to keep the egg warm in a process called **incubation**. The egg is too large for either parent to sit on. Instead, they put one wing over the egg and cuddle it close to their body. The underside of the wing has a patch where the feathers are thin, allowing the puffin's warm skin to press directly against the egg.

It can take anywhere from five to eight weeks for the chick inside the egg to develop. After this time, it begins to **hatch**, tapping at the inside of the eggshell. Eventually, up to three days later, the puffin chick manages to push its way out. The new arrival is covered in fluffy brown feathers called **down**.

Early Days

From its very first day outside its shell, the new chick keeps its parents busy. The chick has no trouble eating small fish whole and eagerly guzzles everything the adults bring. For the first few days, one parent stays with the chick to keep it warm while the other goes fishing. But before long, the chick's appetite is so big that it takes both parents to satisfy it. Load after load of fish is carried into the burrow. The parents emerge a few minutes later, empty beaked. The chick eats at least its own weight in food every day— sometimes 50 or more fish. Not surprisingly, the chick grows fast. After about six weeks it is roughly the size of its parents.

A fluffy puffin chick waits for its parents to bring it food.

A red fox has caught and killed a Pacific horned puffin.

Puffins in Peril

Puffins usually nest on islands, for good reason. Islands have fewer egg-eating predators, such as foxes, stoats, and rats. But even on islands, puffins have plenty of enemies. Birds of prey, such as eagles and falcons, can swoop down to grab puffins from the land or air. Large gulls and crows can fly in to raid puffin burrows, and otters sometimes come ashore to snack on puffin chicks. There's not much the adult puffins can do about these attacks. If the egg is taken soon after it is laid, the female lays another. But if a well-grown chick is killed, the parents do not produce another egg until the following year.

Left Alone

The young puffin's life changes suddenly when it reaches six weeks old. One day, its parents leave the burrow and don't come back. The youngster waits patiently for a while, but after five or six days it seems to realize it has been abandoned. Its instincts tell it to go find out where all those fish its parents brought home came from.

Very sensibly, the young puffin waits until dark, then stumbles out of the burrow. It doesn't know where it is going and soon finds itself at the edge of the cliff. Not knowing any better, it jumps. But its wings are not yet strong enough to fly, so it falls—all the way to the bottom! Fortunately, young puffins are hardly ever hurt by the fall. In no time, they are swimming on the sea with all the other puffins.

At around six weeks old, a puffin chick finds itself on its own.

At summer's end,
all the puffins leave
their cliff-top homes
and take to sea.

All at Sea

While the young puffin, or fledgling, is making
its first dramatic exit from the burrow, its parents
are swimming in the sea below. At this time, like
their baby, the parents cannot fly either. They
have cast off their old flight feathers and are
waiting for the new ones to grow. This process
is called **molting**, and it happens every year.

Over the next few weeks, the young puffins
become strong and skillful enough to catch their
own fish. They also learn to fly. Then, in late
summer, all puffins, young and old, disappear.
The once-crowded cliffs that echoed to their
calls are silent. All that remains are hundreds
of empty burrows. The puffins have returned
to their wintering grounds far, far out to sea.
Some puffins even cross the oceans to Europe
or Asia. The young stay at sea for two or three
years before returning to land in spring. But the
adults come back the next spring to breed again.

Testing Times

In some places where puffins were once very common, the colonies have become much smaller or even disappeared. That is worrisome because it means something about the place must have changed. Sometimes the reason is that there is no longer enough food to be found. That can happen naturally if ocean currents change. But usually people are to blame for the change. If fishers catch too many small fish, there are not enough left in the oceans to support the puffins.

Another problem is predators. Most of the islands where puffins nest have few natural predators. But humans sometimes introduce, or bring, animals such as rats and foxes, which love to eat eggs, to the lands that puffins inhabit.

Finding enough fish to survive is sometimes a problem for puffins.

Look closely and you'll see that this puffin has a metal ring around its leg.

Puffins with Rings

Ornithologists are scientists who study birds. To find out where birds go when they cannot be seen, ornithologists sometimes catch them and put special metal rings on their legs. Each ring has a number on it. Other ornithologists who see the bird later can use that number to find out where the bird has come from. Puffins that have been ringed in places such as the United Kingdom have turned up in Canada, Greenland, and the Mediterranean. They probably don't fly all this way—some puffins may bob on the water, hitching a ride on ocean currents.

Everyone's Favorite

It seems everyone loves puffins, and many people make special trips to the birds' breeding colonies to watch them.

People want to help these birds in places where they are becoming rare. Often, the cliffs where puffins nest are turned into nature preserves. Sometimes whole islands are turned into preserves, and rats and other predators are removed to help the puffins. But, if there are not enough fish in the oceans nearby, the puffins still struggle. It is up to governments to ban fishing in certain areas so that stocks of certain fish can build up again. That is the only way to make sure that there are enough fish for both people and puffins in the future.

Words to Know

Auks Members of the bird family Alcidae, including puffins, guillemots, and murrelets.

Colonies Groups of puffins living in the same place.

Courting When male and female animals spend time together before mating.

Down Small, soft, fluffy feathers that cover a chick, and in adult birds serve as warm under feathers.

Hatch To break out of an egg.

Hemisphere Half of the world. The southern hemisphere includes Antarctica, Australia, Africa, and South America. The northern hemisphere is the other half, including North America, Europe, and Asia.

Incubation	The period between egg laying and hatching, when the eggs must be kept warm.
Mate	Either member of an animal pair; to come together to produce young.
Molting	When birds or animals shed their feathers or fur at certain times of the year.
Ornithologists	Scientists who study birds.
Species	The scientific word for animals of the same type that can breed together.
Streamlined	Describes a smooth, sleek shape that moves through water or air easily.
Trespasser	An animal or person that enters an area that is occupied by others.
Webbed feet	Feet that have skin stretched between the toes.

Find Out More

Books

Crossley, R., K. K. and M. O'Brien. *The Shorebird Guide*.
Boston, Massachusetts: Houghton Mifflin, 2006.

Gaston, A. J. *Seabirds: A Natural History*. New Haven,
Connecticut: Yale University Press, 2004.

Web sites

Everything About Puffins
*birding.about.com/od/birdspuffins/Birds_Everything_
About_Puffins.htm*
Many photographs plus information about where
and how puffins live and make their nests.

Project Puffin
puffin.bird.audubon.org/puffins.html
Learn all about puffins and watch video clips.